DESIGN

REMIX

DESIGN REMIX

A NEW SPIN ON TRADITIONAL ROOMS

COREY DAMEN JENKINS

Foreword by JAMIE DRAKE

RIZZOLI
NEW YORK

New York Paris · London · Milan

I dedicate this first book to every hopeful child of color
who dreams of designing the world. The doors
have been opened, and we are eagerly awaiting your
arrival. Always remember that no one can
make you feel inferior without your permission.

"Race is something you run . . . and win."

—LOLITA CHANDLER

CONTENTS

FOREWORD

COREY DAMEN JENKINS is a man of enormous confidence and great style. The peacock has historically been a symbol of renewal and immortality, and in ancient mythology its tail is seen as having the "eyes" of the stars. I think of Corey, and his work, as this gorgeous bird in the best sense. Personally, he is imposing and serene yet full of vivacity. Likewise, the spaces he designs are restful yet deliciously piquant, always with a daring touch of boldness—or quite a few—added assuredly into his schemes. The plumage of the peacock is filled with aquamarine, chartreuse, fir, forest, and olive, colors that often appear in Corey's gorgeous palettes.

The layering in Corey's work is brought to life through his skilled use of patterns, trims, and details. A racing stripe of passementerie or contrasting fabric is the ornament on many a chairback or fauteuil arm. The ceilings in his spaces are never just another plane: instead, they are lavished with pattern, sheen, or color to lift the eye heavenward. Symmetry is key to his compositions, but foliate patterns soften rigidity.

In 2017 I was seated next to Corey at a dinner during High Point market, hosted by *Traditional Home* magazine. The editor-in-chief was giving a toast, and I leaned over to Corey and stated that I realized that he had become the first African American designer to get the front cover, and that the significance of that historic moment wasn't lost on me. What a breakthrough, for Corey as a black and gay man, and for *Traditional Home*.

From the start, I have always been attracted to Corey's suaveness. His projects capture this same quality. With a great respect for traditional design and antiques, he never veers off track into the staid and stolid, always transporting the elements of history into the current time, imparting a sense of surprise and high-octane energy to the familiar, and reinventing our expectations. And by utilizing antiques in refreshing ways, Corey shows us how the best can be timeless and immortal, respecting the past but living totally in the here and now.

JAMIE DRAKE

779

FROM THE TIME I WAS A CHILD, I've seen the world in color and geometry. I'm the oldest of three boys and, as my mother says, the only one who could always dress himself: I could match, I could mix, I could pattern-play. I have always been very close to my mother, so I copied all the things she did—putting together outfits, playing with color—and loved to surprise and impress her with my style when I came downstairs in the morning. When I got older and my brothers got into sports, I would go with them to their basketball games, but I couldn't have cared less about what was going on on the court. Instead, I paid attention to the architectural elements of the gymnasiums: the angles of the bleachers, the geometry of the lines on the floors.

Another anecdote: When I was three years old, my family had this set of black wrought-iron dining chairs that fascinated me. I was so drawn to these chairs that when no one was looking, I would crawl underneath them and unscrew each seat from its base with my fingers. So then when my parents had friends over, people would fall through the frames because I had made them so loose! This kept happening over a period of months, until one day I got

caught—because I could not stay away from them! This obsession with furniture, and in particular the construction of furniture, has been with me ever since. In addition to the more superficial design elements that I am most known for—bold color, pattern mixing, eclectic arrangements of furniture and decor elements—I take great care in how things are put together. I'm a Detroit boy; I like to get in under the hood.

As I became an adult, I retained all of that focus and aptitude for style and design, but I hid it to a certain degree, because I was told—and told myself—that there was no place for me in this profession. Becoming a starving artist wasn't an option in the family I grew up in. No one was going to bail me out financially or encourage me to follow my dreams into a field that seemed impossible for me to succeed in. So I swallowed those dreams and landed a job as a purchasing agent for a Big Three auto company—a position that was a compromise between my dreams of being an interior designer and my father's insistence that I forge a more traditional path. If I didn't have the creative role I had dreamed of since childhood, I did get to work with contractors, manage budgets, and make big decisions. I had power and stability, the approval of my finance and banking-centric family, and a salary that afforded me a beautiful black luxury sedan, groceries from Whole Foods, a great wardrobe, and a condo in the upscale neighborhood of Rochester Hills, Michigan.

And that all worked just fine until 2008. In the wake of the Great Recession, the city of Detroit

PREVIOUS PAGE: Bold is beautiful. OPPOSITE: Me on the streets of Detroit, my hometown, surrounded by color! Music is a big inspiration in Detroit and on my work. I often use the language of music to describe my design—harmony in pattern play, which element is the soloist and which are the backup singers—and call my approach "design remixed."

CLOCKWISE FROM TOP LEFT: My grandparents supported my interests from the very beginning; here I am drawing in their living room (in a colorful sweater I chose, naturally), 1982. The infamous orange sunglasses! And even at two years old, you would often find me with a pencil in my hands, 1979. My beloved grandparents, Detroit, 1982. **OPPOSITE:** An original sketch from the portfolio I used during my door-to-door campaign.

was broken, and so was I. My beloved hometown, the hometown of my mother and her parents, had been hit hard by the financial crisis, and its downfall was swift and severe—as was mine. I lost my job, and my lifestyle had been reduced to a budget rental apartment, some lonely cans of Spam and SpaghettiOs, and the luxury sedan was traded in for a 1995 white Honda Accord with orange (read: rust) accoutrements. However, I still had those interior-design dreams.

My plan was simple: Find doors, go knock on them. I told myself that I would knock until I found someone to hire me to design their home or hit one thousand rejections—whichever came first. I had taken a map of Detroit and zeroed in on neighborhoods with the biggest, nicest houses. Every day, I set out with my makeshift portfolio of student and charity work, a smile, and a loaner Chrysler 200 from a local Enterprise Rent-A-Car that I had made a deal with: I'd get the same vehicle, at the same rate, each time I went canvassing. (Because that Honda Accord was not going to cut it in the most affluent areas of Motor City.)

But this was still peak Great Recession, so not the time when many potential clients were inclined to undergo a home renovation, especially not, it turned out, one by someone they didn't know who had no previous residential work to speak of. And then there was the color of my skin: I didn't look like the interior designers they had seen in magazines and on TV. I had doors slammed in my face, was chased off of property by dogs, was laughed at by builders when I asked if there was a designer attached to the project they were working on, and was even called "boy" once by an elderly lady. In addition to homes, I went to offices, lobbies, and any commercial space that looked remotely dated. I did this for months until, seven hundred doors in, voices of doubt, hopelessness, and criticism started coming to me at night, and I was too demoralized to ignore them. They told me that I was being foolish and impractical, and that I should stay in my lane—there's no one in interior design who looks like me, so why should I think I could be different? I dialed down my door limit to eight hundred; there was always Starbucks.

AND THEN I CAME TO THE 779TH DOOR.

"A gentle word opens an iron gate." This Bulgarian proverb is now dear to me. Door number 779 was actually behind a pair of wrought iron gates that, once opened, led me to a polite, welcoming

There's a saying here:
Detroit hustles harder.
We are comeback kids,
and whenever we get
knocked down,
we always get back up.

couple in need of a designer. They invited me in for tea—the first time in my hundreds of doors that anyone had done so. They had fired their designer, and after my presentation, they seemed genuinely excited to work with me. Right after the new year— the longest holiday week of my life—they gave me the job and a sizable budget to work with. I decorated the entire house and put photos up on the GoDaddy website that I designed myself (because of course I couldn't afford a webmaster). Then I waited again.

A couple of weeks later, a casting director at HGTV left me a message: They had seen my website, liked my work, and were looking to diversify the cast of one of their design-competition shows. And what did I do? I didn't call him back. Those voices of the night were ringing in my ears again: Who did I think I was? This was fantasy, not a sustainable career. The casting director called a second time, then a third, after which he left me this annoyed message: "I've got a really amazing

BELOW: Some of my favorite architecture in downtown Detroit includes iconic Woodward Avenue (*left*); the Wayne County Building (*center*); the Guardian Building (*right*). **OPPOSITE:** Eastern Market, an area filled with a medley of mom-and-pop shops and other independent vendors, showcases our hometown pride.

opportunity for you, and it would behoove you to call me back."

And that's when I did—and when I kicked those night voices out of my head for good. I thought that if I could knock on eight hundred doors, why not try knocking on millions of doors—every Monday night at 9 p.m.—and take this chance to show a larger audience what I could do? I competed, I won, and that exposure led to more jobs and enough clients for me to launch my own business in Detroit and eventually enough work in the Northeast to open a second office in New York City. But it was all thanks to door number 779 and the fact that I knocked on enough doors to get there.

THERE'S A SAYING HERE: Detroit hustles harder. We are comeback kids, and whenever we get knocked down, we always get back up. So when the city fell, I fell along with it, but we both rose with renewed energy, determination for success, and confidence that we could defy expectations.

Detroit is famously diverse, racially and ethnically, and full of influences from all over the world. We're also incredibly proud of what we've contributed to the American landscape and industry. I'd like to say that my interior-design philosophy pays homage to those two pillars of my native city: my desire to be vibrant and strong, and my instinct to mix colors, shapes, and sizes in a way that is durable and livable, and that redefines—or rather, remixes—classic.

I'm so excited to share my design philosophy with you in this, my first book, as well as the tips, tricks, and answers to the questions I get most frequently. I want to help you create a home with a sophisticated mix by showing you how to use (and love) bold colors, how to create dramatic contrast by mixing patterns and geometry, how to make a statement with neutrals, how to translate fashion inspiration into your home, and much more. But let me start by giving you one piece of advice not for design, but for life: Don't listen to those voices in the night.

THE BOLD
STANDARD

WHERE I COME FROM, BEING BOLD HAS A BIT OF A REPUTATION. In Michigan, being toned down and making safe choices in fashion and design are the norm; a bit of flair is not really part of the lingua franca. ♜ I don't entirely disagree—bold simply for the sake of being bold comes off as hollow and ungrounded. But throughout the history of design—think Classical Florentine, Rococo, and the chintz-loving work of one of my heroes, the great maximalist Mario Buatta—artists and designers have created enticing, memorable, and meaningful visual stories through bold palettes and ornate inspirations. The boldness I love has a backbone of tradition, in which tried-and-true, unassailable architectural elements and decor—"the standards"—are enlivened with striking color, vibrant pattern, and unexpected combinations. It is a point of view that, if done right, is the opposite of trendy. Boldness keeps an older style looking fresh and modern. ♜ The first step to beautiful boldifying is color. Finding bright and unorthodox shades, using them to create unexpected palettes, and then applying those colors and palettes to decor elements in surprising ways is a great approach to any room. For inspiration, I frequently look to fashion magazines and runways, as you can find daring color stories in the fashion world that can be translated to interiors for a fresh but sophisticated look. Once I've selected the colors I want to work with, I think about what architectural elements or pieces of furniture I can apply these colors to that will be pleasing to the eye. I particularly love taking a great architectural detail—a column, molding, or built-in bookcase—that is usually very neutral and

painting it a rich color—turquoise, avocado green—to draw attention to it and give the room as a whole an unexpected jolt.

Materials are another way to go bold. As with color, I also take inspiration from fashion and try to apply ideas I've seen on runways for fabrics and details and bring them into the home. I've upholstered furniture in patent leather, which (in addition to providing a nice, slick sheen) is easy to clean; I've used vibrant wallpapers on the ceilings; and I've added metal trim around a traditional wood floor as an unconventional border. While a striking material may be more subtle than a wall in a saturated color, it can still contribute to a bold look overall by adding depth and texture.

Going bold can also be about making dramatic choices in parts of a house that are usually decorated in more muted ways. Bathrooms, for instance, are typically done in tile and white or pastel colors. But this is the first room many of us see every day, so why not decorate it in a way that will wake—and cheer—you up? This might mean using bolder, richer colors (such as jewel tones or saturated primaries), an intricately patterned wallpaper, or eye-catching pieces of seating or furniture.

Going bold can also be about making dramatic choices in parts of a house that are usually decorated in more muted ways.

PREVIOUS PAGE: The pattern play here is inspired by nature: the wood-grain rug motif, the allusion to waves on the drapes, the sea glass–colored vase, and the flame-stitched upholstery. The Alexia chair is from my collection with Leathercraft. OPPOSITE: A thoughtfully designed guest room signals to friends and family that their presence is valued. This one boasts fifteen-foot-high ceilings and was perfect for bold choices, such as the oversize seeded-glass pendant and floor-to-ceiling drapes in a Greek-key pattern.

Similarly, while whites, neutrals, and washed-out, beachy colors are often used in bedrooms, I love designing bedrooms with bold elements that are personal and positive, to make them spaces that you'll be excited to spend a lot of time in. And incorporating a vibrant mixture of pattern and color into a guest room lets visitors know that their digs are not an afterthought.

Being bold is about playing with what is expected and what has been done before. As a designer, I always want to push my clients exactly to the edge (remember that patent leather?), but not so far that they feel as if they've gone over the cliff of crazy. I take my designs to the limit of where clients feel the exhilaration of the unexpected, while still being grounded in timeless (if dramatically employed) elements. And interestingly, as I've worked bold into my MO, I've discovered that even the most traditional Midwesterners warm quickly to this unconventional approach—they see that winters go faster when you are surrounded with great, bold design!

ABOVE: Don't neglect the wealth of inspiration from eras past. I'm a child of the 1970s, so avocado green is a touchstone. The color definitely raised eyebrows when I suggested it, but a bathroom is the first space that people see in the morning, so why not start your day with a bracing dose of color? **RIGHT:** I chose this wallcovering—a toile from Cole & Son—for similar reasons. The other fun detail in this room is the library by the bathtub. Better to get a book a little wet than an iPad!

LEFT AND ABOVE: I often refer to the ceiling as the "fifth wall." In this dining room, it's covered in a Schumacher wallpaper by Martyn Lawrence Bullard. I turned up the volume on the chair upholstery and window treatments but painted the walls a deep sea blue to keep the room grounded. **FOLLOWING PAGES:** Down with boring bedrooms! People tend to shy away from pattern in rooms where they sleep, so I'm thrilled when I work with someone passionate about color. The peplums on the window treatments in the owners' suite are one of my signatures—their layering lets me combine color, pattern, and passementerie in a vibrant way.

PREVIOUS PAGES: The green wall paint in this foyer and stairwell was custom mixed; I frequently cook up my own color recipes. The focal point is the medley of mirrors in the stairwell, a mix of antique and contemporary—they make the narrow space feel airier. LEFT: The mission for this room was to use the bold walls to highlight—not compete with—the stunning American Colonial Revival architecture, which I achieved with high-gloss white trim and wainscoting. Because the ceilings are only eight feet high, I chose an appropriately scaled pendant rather than a sprawling chandelier.

PREVIOUS PAGES: This room came together in a really fun way. I started with the finishes and worked my way down, so the rug, chosen last, ended up being a synopsis of everything else. The bergères in the foreground are antiques from the early 1900s that I upholstered in white patent leather. I also love the pair of large William and Mary wingbacks in the background, a rare opportunity to use a swath of lemon yellow. LEFT: The custom tête-à-tête draws people into conversation. I designed the bar and the marble floor; the affixed lamps on opposite ends of the bar provide soft ambient light.

PREVIOUS PAGES: I upholstered this antique settee (*right*) in a fun striped fabric and placed it against an iridescent grass-cloth wallcovering to give the room dimension. The antique mirror (*left*) is from a dealer in Detroit. LEFT: Initially, my idea to paint the historic millwork a lacquered navy blue was a hard sell. The traditional approach is to stain millwork or paint it white, but I wanted to celebrate the craftsmanship. The peplums on the window treatments are a multicolored flame-stitched pattern. ABOVE: The wingback chair, almost seven feet tall, commands the corner it sits in. FOLLOWING PAGES: Maritime touches: seascape artwork and a large mirror recalling a ship's porthole. I like making unexpected nods to the passions of each client.

PATTERN HARMONY

The vast landscape—or jungle—of patterns is hard to navigate. Even some designers struggle with it, especially when trying to combine more than one pattern in a single space. There's a very fine line between having just enough and too much going on in a room. The keys to achieving a mix that sings but doesn't shout are thought, planning, rigorous decision making, and the strategies below.

1 | MIND THE SPECS

Geometry, scale, color—these are the characteristics that will make or break a pattern mix. Try to vary the intensity within a room so that each element makes a statement while still coalescing into a single, cohesive visual.

2 | CONTRAST, DON'T COMPETE

Every type of pattern has its own voice. Stripes, for instance, are a mainstay, but they have a a rigidity to them, so I often pair them with plaids or florals—designs that are diametrically opposite to the linear quality of the stripe.

3 | BUILD IN SOME BREAKS

Solids, whether neutral or bold, are great foils for heavy patterns; they help emphasize intricate details in the patterns they coexist with. In a vibrant room, it's good to give the eye a break.

4 | PICK YOUR LEADER

When drafting your pattern story, it's important to choose lead roles and supporting roles. Consider which pattern will be the focal point, then use other patterned accents in more muted, complementary ways.

5 | BE FEARLESS IN YOUR CREATIVITY, BUT JUDICIOUS IN YOUR EXECUTION

When you start planning a room, nothing should be off the table. But when it comes to laying it out, beware of forcing too much into a single space. Successful pattern play means putting on the brakes when you reach that point of harmony, even (or especially) when you want it all.

GOOD BONES

IF YOU'VE GOTTEN THIS FAR IN THE BOOK, YOU KNOW THAT I TAKE a lot of inspiration from my beloved hometown of Detroit. The city, which flourished during the industrial boom of the early twentieth century, has great bones: distinctive architectural influences (particularly art deco) and the unassailable character of such iconic buildings as Albert Kahn's Fisher Building and the Belle Isle Aquarium. Driving around the city really gives you a sense of what has come before you—and an appreciation for that great craftsmanship and handwork of the last century. You know the saying "They don't make them like they used to"? It's a cliché, but it's true. ♕ Yet even though Detroit is an "old" city, it's not nostalgic. An equally powerful quality is its resurgence after a period of decline— how it came back to life with the spirit and underpinnings of what was there before, but with a contemporary flair. We were a mecca of Motown; now we are an electronic- and techno-music epicenter. ♕ I like to channel that spirit of vibrant regeneration—and not merely replication—into a category of homes that have what I call "good bones." These are typically older houses that find themselves in the hands of owners who love them for their history but still need to live in the modern world. To me, the great pleasure of designing one of these houses is that there's already a script for me to work off of. I don't have to invent an architectural story, because an authentic one is baked into the structure of the house: in the wainscoting, the decorative details on banisters, the stained-glass windows. In other words, the trad is there, so my job is to complement it with the nouveau.

But fleshing out those good bones with modern touches can be a puzzle—or perhaps more accurately, a game of Tetris. Older kitchens, for instance, are notoriously tiny by contemporary standards and weren't built to accommodate the sizes and amounts of appliances that are considered standard in a house today. So you can't be *too* precious about the DNA of a space, or else you'll create a home that's beautifully unlivable. Sometimes you need to knock down a wall or two to save a room from its own gravitas, but knowing when—and more importantly where—to stop is key. My rule for figuring out what to keep and what to remove is this: If it ain't broke, don't fix it. So leave the custom moldings and the stained glass, all the beauty and craftsmanship that is so hard to come by these days. But for those things you can't live with, like doorways that are too low to accommodate the height of the owners, surgically remove those elements while allowing the rest of the home's character to thrive.

Trying to understand what drove the original design of a room is also helpful when coming up with a new approach. Lighting technology, for instance, has changed so much over the course of the twentieth century; this means that not only do we have better options for how we illuminate our homes, we also have more options for arranging furniture, since groupings are less dependent upon being centered around limited light sources. Heating and insulation are other examples: if you have central heating, maybe you no longer need

My rule for figuring out what to keep and what to remove is this: If it ain't broke, don't fix it.

PREVIOUS PAGE: A rare instance where I did not paint over dark wood. I showcased the beautiful details by lightening the floors and selecting a bright rug and furniture. **OPPOSITE:** A house from the early 1900s in Summit, New Jersey. I used a geometric pattern on the wood-veneer wallcovering and a modern chandelier to reveal the beauty of the columns and moldings. The unexpected raspberry stair runner gives the foyer impact. **RIGHT:** This lady's office under the stairs had an original stained-glass window; I used a similarly colorful fabric on the desk chair.

those heavy curtains that were once a necessity to keep the cold out during the winter. Instead, try lighter treatments that will showcase the beautiful original pediments of the window. It's a win-win!

Older homes have often been decorated numerous times throughout the decades, so sometimes the original charm is buried under a mishmash of trends and color palettes from various owners. The key in this case is to go back to the source—reclaim the charm of whatever original details remain, then build on them in a way that suits your taste: work in a color story or artwork that feels personal to you, or choose furniture in a style that fits your lifestyle, rather than trying to museum-ify the house with antiques. (Here's a tip: it's usually the "heavier" element—dark-stained paneling, elaborate chandeliers—that drags a room down.)

After tackling the technical challenges and coming up with a strategy for layering the new into the old, the final step is taking a step back to see how it all works. My goal is to create a kind of trompe l'oeil, where the period details mesh with the new touches seamlessly enough that—while certain key elements draw your eye—you might not be able to pinpoint what year the room was designed in. And in this day and age, when so much that is classical is being razed and replaced by new construction, you should take particular satisfaction in giving good bones another try. It's like recycling vintage pieces instead of buying fast fashion: there's depth and implicit longevity in bringing classic homes back to life.

LEFT: Curb appeal is very important to me. The interiors of a well-appointed house should rouse your curiosity as you drive by. In this bay window, I designed bolster pillows the exact width of the window frame, so the area always looks tailored from the driveway. **FOLLOWING PAGES:** An antique mirror is flanked by two 1920s chairs that I re-covered in a flame-stitched pattern (*left*). I love the look of white, sculptural pieces in rooms with a lot of dark wood (*right*).

ABOVE: A gold motif appears in several places, including the brass piping of the table behind the sofa (*left*). The sculpture on the coffee table is made from hand-folded book pages (*right*). **OPPOSITE:** I honored the incredible carved woodwork around the mantel with an oversize antique mirror and a regal Empire-style sconce from my Hudson Valley Lighting collection. **FOLLOWING PAGES:** As much attention as I pay to the ceiling of a room, I never neglect the floor. The bench with acrylic legs appears to float over the Greek key–patterned rug, and I repainted the original ornate plasterwork on the ceiling ivory.

PREVIOUS PAGES: In this house from the mid-1990s, which is made to look historic, I chose a marbleized Schumacher wallpaper to accentuate the curvature of the millwork (*left*). The home is full of American Colonial details—archways, intricate moldings, twisted balusters—that had previously been covered up. So I stripped away the heavy curtains, swags, and jabots and painted the stairs black (*right*). OPPOSITE AND RIGHT: I'm a big fan of a salon-style gallery wall (see page 78), and these spaces represent two different approaches. At left, an eclectic arrangement of gilt-framed artwork livens up a narrow space. Instead of adding sconces, every piece of art has its own picture light. Over the living room sofa, I hung a series of plaster wall brackets, topped with books and scalloped urns for a subtler impact.

PREVIOUS PAGES: More and more people I work with are interested in repurposing pieces they already own, which I love. We remixed nearly thirty pieces of furniture for this space. The coffee table was previously black chinoiserie; I transformed it into a softer element by dipping it in white lacquer. Among the new pieces we custom designed are the two wingback chairs and the double-bolstered ottoman. **ABOVE AND OPPOSITE:** In the owner's suite, heavy drapes were swapped out for café curtains that leave the focus on the windows themselves (*above left*). Details in the owner's suite (*above right and opposite*).

PREVIOUS PAGES: The good bones in this room are definitely the furniture: the four-poster bed, dresser, table, and wardrobe. Because I really wanted those pieces to stand out, I kept everything else simple and light, so details like the pineapples on the bedposts wouldn't get lost. **OPPOSITE:** The Federal-style mirror is grounded by the antique sideboard. A vintage lamp adds a soft, sculptural quality to the mix. **RIGHT:** This ornate sconce is a scene stealer, and I thought it would be fun and lively to use it as a statement above a console. **FOLLOWING PAGES:** The furniture here is a mix of pieces from elsewhere in the house that were re-covered or repainted. I wanted this dining room to be all about drama, so I commissioned high-shine lacquered walls— you can literally do your makeup in them! The tiled fireplace surround is original to the house and drove the color palette for the room.

PREVIOUS PAGES: This project got the nickname "Candy Crush" for its cheery palette of bubblegum pink, lime, and raspberry. **ABOVE AND OPPOSITE:** More candied details, punctuated by a bolster in my beloved yellow and another salon-style hanging featuring some of the owners' heirloom artworks and needlepoint. **FOLLOWING PAGES:** If it ain't broke, don't fix it. We left the original imprint and cabinetry of this kitchen intact but livened up everything with new paint colors, light fixtures, and window treatments.

HOSTING THE SALON

A salon-style hanging is a great way to give a small or overlooked space its own personality. Stairwells, foyers, powder rooms, and breakfast nooks are some of my favorite areas to use this kind of design element—any small space where you want a shot of verve and character. While you can buy pieces with the specific intent to create a salon-style collage, I think these compositions are most successful when they incorporate mementos of significance and pieces that you already own.

1 | CHOOSE YOUR APPROACH

There are two basic directions: uniform, where the frames match and subject matter is consistent (all black-and-white photos or watercolors of the same size); and eclectic, where the frames are different sizes and shapes and there's more of a mix of elements and a looser grid.

2 | THINK OUTSIDE THE FRAME

A salon-style collage is a great way to showcase collections or inherited items like antique mirrors, African masks, mounted plates, or pieces of porcelain. Depending on the approach you choose, you can make a dedicated space for these elements or mix them with others.

3 | PLAN BEFORE YOU HAMMER

Once you've chosen your elements and the space in which you want to hang them, lay everything out on the floor and arrange it there. Be sure to measure the place where the frames will hang and the space between each of the pieces, so you come up with a collage that makes sense for the space before you start putting holes in the wall.

4 | TAKE A BREAK BEFORE YOU COMMIT

After I've created my groupings on the floor and measured everything precisely, I always step away before I start hanging. While nailing the spatial relations is key, your gut will tell you if it's working visually when you look at the final product after a pause.

5 | A LITTLE GOES A LONG WAY

You don't need an extensive art collection, tons of family heirlooms, or a huge stash of antiques. Four or five pieces that have sentimental value collaged together thoughtfully can be more impactful than an entire wall—and easier to put together successfully.

LESS > MORE

I'M AN UNABASHED LOVER OF CLASSIC DESIGN—ELEMENTS THAT have stood the test of time because they have integrity and purpose. But if there's a central tenet to my design philosophy, it isn't tied to any particular style. I believe in principles of design but not rules, because rules confine you to a certain spectrum of tastes, whereas principles let you apply an overarching idea just about anywhere. So when clients come to me, as they often do, saying they would like to work together but that their taste is more modern—read: minimalist—than what they've seen me do before, I'm thrilled to work with them. For those clients who love minimalism and midcentury-modern design, it's all about creating a home where less becomes more. ♟ First, let's define what "less" means in terms of the elements of design. For furniture, it means fewer decorative flourishes, such as carved ball-and-claw foot furniture legs, patterned upholstery, or fluted details, and more strong, clean lines. I choose pieces that make an impact in shape or by the texture of the upholstery rather than the details. For color, it means a pared-down palette and fewer, simpler moments of contrast (though don't remove contrast altogether—more on that in a bit!). For decor, it means more natural-looking materials (wood, jute and sisal rugs, textural stone), smooth surfaces (tile, marble), and fewer accoutrements (like bejeweled chandeliers, trims, or patterned wallpaper). The minimalist approach is for situations where there's a single, clear vision of the design, whether that's from a single owner, or a couple whose tastes are closely aligned. ♟ The most important thing to know when trying a less-is-more

approach in your own home is that you can't be lazy: there are fewer pieces to hide behind. Do you know the journalism adage "Kill your darlings"? The same idea of power in economy—having a high bar for what is extraneous and eliminating everything but the essential—applies here. The goal is to create rooms that feel smooth, concise, well thought out, and deliberate. When starting to design a room, remember that the process is not about creating harmony between a number of contrasting elements. Instead, pick one element to be the soloist or diva—whether that's a color, an eye-catching piece of furniture, or an architectural element like a staircase—and then try to make all of the other elements in the room support it.

Yes, you read that right: when you commit to less, you can still be bold in a different way. In the more public spaces of a house—entryways, living rooms, kitchens—even when I'm doing a "less" design, I believe there should always be some element that gives a wow factor. This is a single note of style that makes the room feel memorable, such as a modern chandelier or light feature, an oversize (but not messy-looking) piece of furniture, bold artwork, or a dramatic kitchen island. Particularly in larger rooms, if there isn't some sort of a statement to pull the room together, the entire design will fall flat. In more intimate spaces, like bedrooms, studies, and bathrooms, instead of a larger element that draws focus, I like to deploy a little

PREVIOUS PAGE: Public spaces, like the lobby of the Michigan Design Center, often call for a less-is more approach.
OPPOSITE: This room is an example of how less color can still be bold. The umber walls are impactful because of the richness of the hue-you feel like you are being bathed in chocolate when you step into the room. Even the oversize chandelier has a lightness because of its wispy, elegant lines.

The punctuation of color, pattern, and texture can be a tricky thing in most design schemes. A little goes a long way.

bit of pattern or a jolt of color to prevent the space from feeling cold or soulless. There is such a thing as too much neutrality!

Punctuation of color, pattern, and texture can be a tricky thing in most design schemes: a little goes a long way, often further than you think. But counterintuitively, it's almost the opposite in a less-is-more approach. A big wall in a rich, impactful color makes a bolder statement than lots of different colors in multiple smaller areas, which results in a less sleek and more eclectic look. Similarly, a sofa in a luxurious, neutral-colored fabric without any other adornment can command serious reverence, more than if the hand of that material was obscured by a bright color or pattern.

A final note of caution: though the less-is-more approach is correctly associated with a modern sensibility, be wary of drifting toward choices that are trendy or basic. To avoid being over the top, people sometimes take less risk—and fall victim to what is popular, what is easy, and what is bland. "Less" should be as deliberate, and creative, as "more." My only unbreakable rule (OK, principle) is that no matter the style, no matter how much or how little is adorned, you always want to end up with rooms that feel timeless and will stand up to the tastes of today, tomorrow, and beyond.

ABOVE: The kitchen island and backsplash, made of honed quartzite, have a beautiful wavelike pattern that draws you gently into the space. I echoed the reference to nature by showcasing the top cabinets in their natural white oak, then mixed in a touch of glam with gold and silver accents on the light fixtures and vent. **OPPOSITE:** In this dining area, I wanted to make sure the beautifully framed windows did not get lost, so I opted for simple motorized shades. The chairs are covered in a durable navy vinyl.

LEFT: Since I was involved with this project from the construction phase, I had a lot of control over the architectural elements. The ceiling, which features a pattern that I designed, is two-toned, with a taupe-gray base and bright white moldings. The furniture follows this lead, with every piece showing off clean, sculptural lines—even the vases on the coffee table have a sculptural character to them. **ABOVE:** Sometimes I play with pattern, other times with shape. I designed the accordion-styled fireplace mantel to further underscore this room's geometric style.

PREVIOUS PAGES: When you need a straightforward statement that won't overwhelm, you can't go wrong with the combination of navy lacquer and gold, seen here in the lamps and trim on the octagonal mirror (*left*). One of the owners of this house wanted more color than the other, so the host and hostess chairs are upholstered in a vibrant floral print. Otherwise, this room is all about simple, traditional furnishings and details. The ceiling is covered with a navy faux hide, while the walls are wrapped in a soft mint grass cloth (*right*). **LEFT:** I have a sentimental attraction to this starburst chandelier—it reminds of the first movie I ever saw in 1978: *Superman*. **OPPOSITE:** The foyer of this house was relatively small, so I manipulated the wall frames to accommodate a built-in bench. To give this nook its own personality, I covered the wall with a wood veneer and the cushion in a luxurious ostrich leather.

OPPOSITE: A patterned accent wall in a light color, like the one behind the bed, is a great way to bring a touch of vibrancy into a less is-more approach. The glass lamps on the nightstands are vintage. ABOVE: The bench at the foot of the bed is piped in leather, which gives it a retro look. Underneath the ivory drapery panels are roller shades, which provide additional coverage from outdoor light without adding an extraneous design detail.

ABOVE: This wallpaper is very dynamic—full of trees, flowers, and birds—but I was able to work it into a quiet space because the colors are subtle and pale. The armchair is an antique from Sweden, upholstered in a classic tape trim that I'm fond of using.
OPPOSITE: I went for a very spa-like color palette in this owners' bathroom. The floors are a combination of marble and porcelain with a custom inlaid geometric pattern. Two vintage dressers were converted into his-and-hers vanities.

OPPOSITE: One thing I love best about a less-is-more approach is that when subtracting color and pattern play, shapes and geometric details—like the chunky, scalloped legs of this desk—really have a chance to shine. It's also an opportunity to get creative with texture, like the three-dimensional art across from the desk. **ABOVE:** An owner's bathroom that needed nothing more than marble, stone, and clean lines.

THE ART OF THE SHELF

I am always drawn to bookshelves in any home, no matter what's on them. To me, their intrigue isn't about checking out someone's reading habits—it's the unique quality of the space itself, which can house all sorts of different aesthetic choices and design elements. In other words, I like to think of bookshelves not as a place to store the things you read, but rather as a place to showcase the things you love.

1 | BOOKS ARE OPTIONAL

If you haven't yet amassed the book collection of your dreams, don't worry— you can bring in other decorative objects to fill in the blanks. As you fill the shelves with tomes you love, you can rearrange accordingly.

2 | A PLACE TO HANG

I often "hang" pieces of art in bookshelves, whether or not they are full of books. The look of a piece of framed art or photography in a shelf has an intriguing and different visual impact than when it's on a wall.

3 | MATCH AND MIX

Bookshelves are great places for small groupings of similar items—think a collection of vases or shells. But within each grouping, it's nice if there's some variety in size and shape.

4 | DON'T FORGET THE SHELVES THEMSELVES

There's no law that says bookshelves have to be white or made from wood. You can paint your shelves or line them with a textured material. In my 2019 Kips Bay showhouse room, I used an emerald-green grass cloth to wrap the interior of the bookshelves.

5 | OR LOSE THE SHELVES ALL TOGETHER

If you don't have a library's worth of shelves, be creative. Étagères, freestanding cabinets, and credenzas can also serve as display spaces, especially in apartments and smaller homes.

ECLECTIC EXUBERANCE

I ALWAYS SAY THAT I HAVE AN APPRECIATION FOR EVERY DESIGN style—from traditional to modern and everything in between—and it's true. But if you want to know what any interior designer really loves, all you have to do is take a look at their own living spaces. And my home is an expression of a design approach that I call "eclectic exuberance." ♜ I use the term *design approach* rather than *style* because one of the things that makes eclectic exuberance so appealing is that it lets you pick the things you love (as many as you want!) and gives you permission to combine them outside the design norms. There is no strict list of dos and don'ts, like a certain color palette or level of ornamentation. It is a great approach for someone who is passionate about travel, history, and other cultures, because it allows—mandates, really—you to celebrate diversity and tap into an adventurous spirit. ♜ I know what you are thinking: That all sounds great, Corey, but you can't just throw all sorts of things together and magically have a great room, right? Actually, you can. My strategy when I decorated my own Michigan home and New York City apartment, and when I'm doing homes for other exuberantly eclectic clients, is less like writing a recipe— adding this amount of antiques, then a dash of contemporary art—and more like throwing everything into the blender, pushing the ON button, and seeing what I create. I love the challenge of combining design ingredients that aren't supposed to go together. It's invigorating and inspiring to come up with new combinations, but after that initial round of mixing things, the trick is how you tweak

the various elements to get to a point where there's harmony in the disparity.

Let's say you love pattern: animal prints, stripes, paisleys, or anything but a solid color. Great! Invite them all in. But then you need to figure out a hierarchy, essentially assigning a visual value to each of the patterns you want to play with. If a leopard print is more important to you than a multicolored stripe, maybe that becomes the pattern for a piece of upholstery or a rug; stripes can appear on accent pillows in muted hues. Make a deliberate decision on the big pieces first, then work your way down to the smaller details. Turning down the volume on other design aspects helps too—keeping the color palette modest and not going crazy with textures. And then it's crucial in these types of spaces that you find places for the eyes to rest: bare walls, neutral floorcoverings, or simple line drawings as artwork. The last thing you want to do as an interior designer is give someone vertigo in his or her own home!

If all of this sounds intriguing but a little intimidating, you can start small. Maybe instead of combining all of your design proclivities in a room, you can focus on creating an eclectic statement in one part of it, like arranging treasures and accessories on a mantel or creating a vibrant salon-style wall. (See sidebar on page 78.)

A cool thing about this approach is that it lets you consider and deploy pieces that don't quite

I love the challenge of combining design ingredients that aren't supposed to go together— it's invigorating and inspiring to come up with new combinations.

make sense on their own—they are too odd, different, or loud to be a traditional focal point—but when used in combination, they have a beautiful visual flow. There's an antique Ming chair in the entry of my apartment that I love for its unusually tall size; it doesn't "go" with anything else in the house in a traditional sense, but when paired with a stack of decorative boxes and a piece of abstract art, it commands a small corner of the home in an interesting, eye-catching way. This approach is also great for people like me, who will never give up classical elements—things like chinoiserie or carved wood—because it lets you moderate the potential stuffiness of older, antiquated styles with things like contemporary art and modern furniture.

What I love about eclectic exuberance is how positive it is, and how empowering: it's OK to like a lot of things, and it's OK to have taste that is busy sometimes and sleek at others. Also, there's an authenticity to this approach to decorating. People come to it because of individual pieces or elements that they are genuinely attracted or attached to— not because they are trying to mold their taste into a single style. Eclectic exuberance is about having it all in joyful moderation.

PREVIOUS PAGES: This client was a real fashionista and could never have too much pattern play in her home! Therefore, the objective for this living room was to capture her spirit without going overboard. I carved out interesting places for the eye to rest: the solid-colored velvet sofa; the modern, clean-lined cocktail table; and the white walls with high-gloss black trim on the doors and mantel.

RIGHT: The natural world is alive in this breakfast nook, which has a hand-painted garden scene and a gilded branch pendant.

PREVIOUS PAGES: I always try to sell my clients on yellow, especially the ones who live where winters can be gray. The decor is from eclectic sources—the lamp on the right-hand page is from Africa and the mirror is from the 1940s. **ABOVE:** The salon-style arrangement in my Michigan home features a variety of pieces that are meaningful to me. I created interesting juxtapositions between size, shape, medium, and color. **OPPOSITE:** The living room of my condo features what I think of as controlled pattern and texture play. The wing chair is in a funky, colorful Kravet fabric.

WORLD HISTORY

The Meaning of Home | JEFFREY ALAN MARKS

INSPIRED DESIGN

欲窮千里目
更上一層樓

白日依山盡
黄河入海流

PREVIOUS PAGES: In the entry, I paired this hand-painted chinoiserie credenza with a piece of contemporary art by Antonio Pulgarin (*left*). This brass bar trolley was the first piece of antique furniture I ever bought (*right*). LEFT: The repetition of blue and white porcelain throughout the dining room helps ground the eclectic mix of artwork and other personal mementos. OPPOSITE: This antique dining table from Belgium was lost at sea for six months but worth the wait: I love the carved legs, the audacious heaviness of it—it truly commands the space. FOLLOWING PAGES: This might come as a surprise, but I prefer a darker, more toned down color story in the bedroom (*left*). You can still have big personality in a small space. The turquoise-and-gold hexagonal wallpaper livens up a bathroom in my condo (*right*).

ABOVE, OPPOSITE, AND FOLLOWING PAGES: For clients who had been living abroad for many years, an eclectic approach allowed me to draw on all sorts of mementos from their travels within the Tuscany-inspired palette they loved. I appreciated the old-world inspiration, but to bring the room into the present, I layered in some jolts of terra-cotta and aquamarine and a few touches of modernity, like geometric throw pillows and a piece of abstract art over the mantelpiece.

OPPOSITE: While all of my projects are dear to me, this one holds a special place in my heart since this is the owners' bedroom behind door number 779! I still remember every detail, and I love that my approach has remained consistent since they gave me my big break. ABOVE: The bed frame is upholstered in velvet, the sconces are polished nickel, and the patterns mix ikat, geometric, and stripe. This couple used to live by the water in Massachusetts, so I chose a palette that was earthy but mixed the colors of the sea, beach sunsets, and sand.

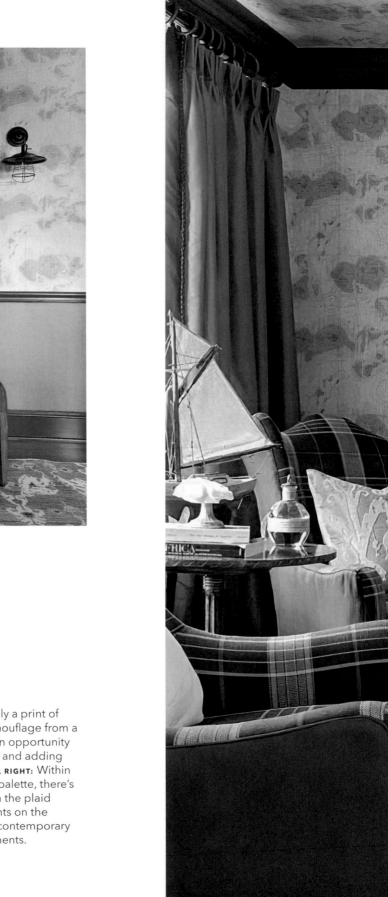

ABOVE: The wallpaper in this study is actually a print of old world maps, though it can read as camouflage from a distance. I used the chair-rail molding as an opportunity for more mixing by painting it rusty brown and adding a houndstooth-print wallcovering below it. **RIGHT:** Within this room's chocolate, crème, and currant palette, there's a lot going on: note the leather accents on the plaid chairs, which contrast with the wood accents on the leather chair, and the juxtaposition of the contemporary art piece against the more traditional elements.

LEFT: The furnishings in the living room are a mix of antiques, such as the chair and ottoman (*top*), and custom-made pieces, like the oversize coffee table (*below*). A large table gives you the opportunity to create an eclectic decorative arrangement. **OPPOSITE:** A room with twenty-foot-high ceilings needs some variety to keep the decor from feeling monotonous. The walls, which are painted in a color called Applesauce Cake by PPG Paints, are broken up by a honeyed hue on the ceiling, sage and kelly green accents, and the plaid of the rug.

STYLE CUES

Fashion is the way that I take my clients' temperatures on a lot of design issues. If I see they wear a lot of patterns or have an affinity for a certain type of tailoring or silhouette, those preferences become starting points for my own brainstorming. Here are ways to use your personal style in clothing to make inspired design choices in the home.

1 | THINK ABOUT TOUCH

In addition to colors and prints, be creative about materials and textures you like to touch and wear. I've hung chandeliers with leather straps and used silk on window treatments.

2 | CONSIDER DROPPING IT IF IT'S HOT

Scrutinize trends before bringing them into your home. It's one thing to use fashion to discover something you love; it's another to get swept up in the zeitgeist and bring in elements that will look trite or dated as soon as the moment passes.

3 | TRANSLATE THE BLING

Those who love jewelry, sparkle, and shine can nod to that in their homes by adding metallic accents and making bigger statements with hardware. I also use glass and crystal boxes and fabrics with a sheen to create a similar effect.

4 | CAST A WIDE NET

While looking at the clothes you own is a good place to start, fashion inspiration doesn't have to be limited to your closet. Do some research with magazines, runway images, and style blogs to look for ideas that maybe you wouldn't wear yourself, but you'd be excited to see every day in your home.

5 | TOGETHERNESS HAS LIMITS

It's rare that both people in a couple have the same taste. So when partners or spouses have really opposing styles, I divide each set of preferences. Then I apply them where they make sense, instead of trying to appease them both in every room. That way, everyone's taste gets to shine.

NIGHT & DAY

MY FIRST DESIGN OFFICE HAD A NEUTRAL COLOR PALETTE punctuated by bright emerald-green walls. It was a beautiful space—one that expressed my love for brightening traditional design with bold touches—but I found that the longer I was there, the more green dominated my thoughts, which is not helpful when you are running a business that relies on your ability to think in every color of the rainbow! So when it came time to move into a new work space, I opted for a color story of black and white. There was nothing simple about it, though. I played up patterns, contrasting tones, textures, and finishes, and I added glamour with gold nailhead trim and cremone bolts on the bar cabinet. The office is now chic, but not timid—a good example of my belief that taking a break from color doesn't have to mean taking a break from bold. ♕ As a design approach, "night and day" is about more than color, or the lack thereof. It's really about how making one choice—committing to the most classic of color combinations—allows you to throw your creative energy into other aspects of design. This approach offers some of the most exciting opportunities for pattern play, because reducing the number of characters in your color story makes it possible to mix multiple patterns—geometrics, stripes, animal prints, toiles, Greek keys—in one space without it feeling too busy. It's also a great opportunity to let metallics like gold, silver, brass, and chrome really shine. Reflective elements take on the tones and effects around them, so when paired with black and white, they add richness and luxury to the overall aesthetic. ♕ On the other hand, the black-and-white approach can also act

as a stage on which to showcase an additional saturated color whose impact would be drowned out if used in a space with lots of competing hues. For example, I don't often use red in my work—it's an energetic color that doesn't always play nice with other design elements. Yet when positioned against a strong but not showy foundation, a red piece of furniture or design element can provide a singular point of focus that brings the room together. Other primary colors also play well off black (or other dark hues) and white, as do jewel tones. In that first design office, the reason that emerald was so captivating was because I had played it off of black, white, and gold. A night-and-day scheme is also great for highlighting colorful artwork.

You'll notice, however, that this chapter is called "Night & Day" rather than "Black & White." There is actually quite a tonal variety within the broader categories of whites and blacks (and navy), which can add great dimension to your space if used thoughtfully but also trip up people if they don't pay attention to subtle variations. While snow white works well in some cases—tile in bathrooms or kitchens, for instance—I often steer my clients toward cream or ivory when it comes to paint colors and furniture, because those tones are more welcoming to other elements in the room. One trick of the trade is to paint the walls a few shades warmer than pure white, because pure white can

PREVIOUS PAGE: All of the furnishings here are from my Leathercraft collection; the skirted tête-à-tête in the center is called Gwendolyn, after my mother, to honor her as a woman of balance and the elegant, mediating force among her husband and three sons. OPPOSITE: I replaced the emerald-green walls in my Detroit office with a Moroccan-inspired pattern in black and ivory, so the room still feels vibrant, but visitors don't feel like one color will dominate their thoughts.

An ivory-and-onyx approach is evergreen, with infinite possibilities for reinvention.

make neutral-colored elements look dingy by contrast. So save that pure white for trims and accents. It's important to remember that white, ivory, cream, and ecru are all distinct colors, and while they can live together in a room, the approach is more mixing than matching. Similarly with blacks, you want to be mindful of the richness and the finishes, again remembering that a matte black and an onyx lacquer have very different visual notes, especially when light hits them.

When it comes to alternatives to black, navy or midnight blue provides a softer "night" effect. I have used an inky shade of blue on bedroom walls, which is more calming than black but still is conducive to sleep. This "soft night" effect is also present in dark neutral colors, such as charcoal gray, and shades of umber and espresso.

A night-and-day approach is evergreen, with infinite possibilities for reinvention. For this reason, it's great to use in rooms that see a lot of traffic, like commercial spaces and offices, places where you don't want a specific color choice to literally color people's overall impression. When done right, this high-contrast style draws the eye more deeply into subtle details—the careful mixing of finishes and textures, the nuanced contrasting of trims—touches that take a room from purely functional into the realm of wow.

RIGHT: The absence of bold color means that I have room to showcase my favorite textures, like wicker and leather. The bar cabinet, designed by yours truly, is covered in white leather; the cremone bolts add another textural element.
FOLLOWING PAGES: An architecturally stunning entryway becomes even more dramatic when crimson is deployed against a black-and-white backdrop (*left*). Two-story spaces can make for a powerful first impression, especially with a bold, graphic wallcovering. The channel-back sofa facilitates conversation when people are arriving or leaving (*right*).

LEFT: I love letting the color red work its magic in my designs. Here, we continued the crimson accents from the foyer into the living room. OPPOSITE: I prefer separate groupings of seating areas rather than one long sectional; it lets me create a design mix, and it's also more responsive to how people actually live. (Have you ever been to a party where the guests wanted to be in the same conversation all night?) Conversation nooks, like those next to the bookshelves, are visually intriguing and also foster a more varied living atmosphere. And if you don't have enough books to fill up shelves across a long room, they are an alternative use of space. FOLLOWING PAGES: The crimson Lacanche range makes the kitchen come alive (*left*). At the end of the kitchen island, I built in breakfast-nook seating with a channel back to create a continuous flow from food preparation to family time (*right*).

OPPOSITE: In the dining room, I removed the red to give the space a look of cool, clean contrast. By rendering it in black and white, even a traditional floral wallcovering gets a modern touch. **ABOVE:** I'm always looking for ways to pack in texture, and the mesh crowns on these chandeliers do just that—when the light goes on, they filter the rays across the ceiling in a kaleidoscopic effect. But the real showstopper is the room's tin ceiling, which we designed for this project.

LEFT: The Moroccan pattern on the kitchen island doesn't bring in a lot of extra color, but the geometric energy of it makes the room fun to be in, as does the mixing of black and white paints on the cabinetry. **ABOVE:** Instead of limiting a backsplash to just the area right behind a sink or range, I like to add drama by doing one fluid wall treatment from countertop to ceiling. This one is made entirely of quartzite.

ABOVE: When making big graphic statements in opposing colors like black and white, symmetry and repetition can prevent the space from becoming chaotic. On the walls of this owner's bathroom are two disparately scaled patterns—one oversize, the other reduced—which, along with the looser geometric floral on the floor, play with scale in an interesting way. **OPPOSITE:** It's rare that I keep a ceiling plain white, but in this case, it allowed me to do a bold black trim and gave the vibrant wallcovering room to breathe. I integrated the navy of the velvet settee by using pillows that united all three colors.

OPPOSITE: I used cremone bolts on the cabinetry by this breakfast nook to make them more interesting without adding color. The bolts are typically used on French doors; I also used them on the bar cabinet in my office on pages 140–41. The walls show that even simple subway tiles can become a textural element that enlivens white walls. **ABOVE:** In this kitchen, I used a navy blue as my "night," so the feeling is more midnight than black. The brass on the range, hood, and pendants gives a jolt of brightness.

While I often say that you need to pick the "lead singer" in every design scheme, you can sometimes accommodate a duet. This family room is anchored by two powerful design statements: the bold Greek-key pattern on the Stark rug and the vibrant goldenrod sofa, with all of the other elements playing a supporting role. The walls and ceiling are painted the same champagne color, which flows seamlessly from the floor up. In rooms without a crown molding, painting the walls and ceiling the same color makes the space feel larger.

PREVIOUS PAGES: My favorite detail about this room is the unusual black and white inset trims on the wall. They give the walls a tailored quality, which I contrasted with pieces such as the ornate 1920s coffee table. **ABOVE:** The entry table is usually the first element people engage with in a home. Here, I chose a table where most of the drama was in the base. **RIGHT:** People are often afraid that white furniture will quickly look dirty, but it won't if you choose your materials wisely. The top of this table skirt is made of ostrich vinyl, which can be easily wiped down.

LEFT: My inspiration for this breakfast nook was a table for two at a Paris café. I chose a chrome bistro table because I wanted something inviting that added atmosphere to the room. **FOLLOWING PAGES:** The owner wanted a posh, hotel-like experience in her bathroom. (In fact, she called me after a stay at a luxurious hotel to tell me that she thought her bathroom at home was nicer than theirs—music to an interior designer's ears!) The custom vanity was painted cobalt blue, and I felt like the room needed a touch of whimsy to temper the stark color and geometry, so I chose mirrors with an organic bird motif (*left*). Inside classic marble walls is an inset stone pattern, against which the brass fittings play like jewelry (*right*).

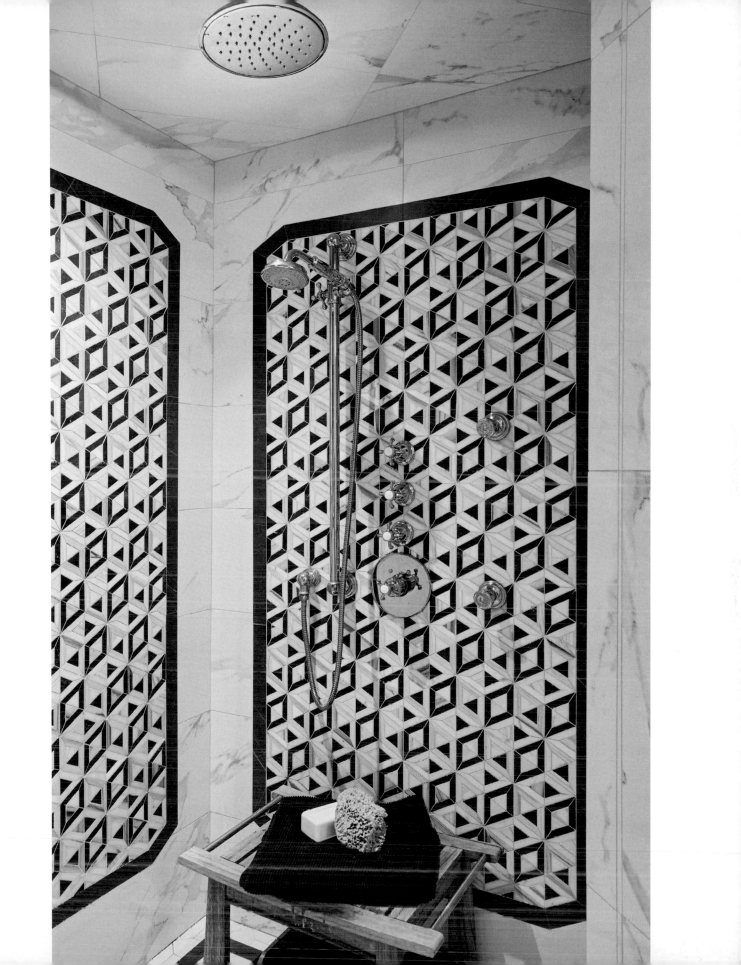

ABOVE: I'm a lover of all things Hollywood Regency—especially when I get to modernize the style for the twenty-first century! Flanked by gilt-wood chinoiserie pagoda mirrors, this four-poster bed is set off by a dramatic pleated-silk treatment. **RIGHT:** The sculptural bed has silver trim on it. I don't often do silver-leafed furniture, but in this case, the subtle accent gave this custom piece a vintage feel.

LEFT: In this loggia, I painted the brick wall a sugary color to serve as a crisp backdrop for the artwork and dark wicker furniture. Some people think wicker looks dated, but I think it can look very handsome—like all classics, it depends on how it's interpreted. The gilt fire screen and contemporary table lamps help it feel modern. FOLLOWING PAGES: The teak dining table brings the natural world into this indoor-outdoor space (*left*). Air plants, like the ones arranged on the shelf behind the lamp, are an easy way to add real greenery to a space (*right*).

COLOR COORDINATION

There's so much to talk about when it comes to paint selection: how to choose between subtle differences in tone and finish (flat or matte paint is great in bedrooms; eggshell is nice and forgiving for kitchens; high-gloss paint belongs on trim) and how not to make yourself crazy trying to match paint colors to furniture. (Answer: You don't need to! These elements don't have to match, they just have to flow.) I also love to use bold paint colors on doors and moldings.

1 | WAIT TO PAINT

There's a natural inclination pick your paint first, then figure out the rest of the room; try it the other way around. There are endless paint colors but more limited choices in furnishings, so it's much easier to select that at the end.

2 | KNOW YOUR LIGHT

Consider the way natural light affects the room, and don't fight it. If your home gets only modest natural light, create a mellower ambience that's warm and inviting instead of going overboard with bright, sparkling elements.

3 | TEST, TEST, AND TEST AGAIN

While you usually have to pay for tester paint, it's worth the investment. (If you do end up using any of the tester colors, save them for touch-ups.) Try several shades, and leave them up for a bit to see how each looks in different lights. Tip: Order your testers in flat paint, rather than high-gloss, which may show through when painted over.

4 | ACCENT THOUGHTFULLY

The purpose of an accent wall is to draw a person's attention, so it's a great opportunity to show off color. But don't just throw bold paint onto any wall. The wall's position and function in the room determines whether it can take a strong swath of color.

5 | GOOGLE IS YOUR FRIEND

If you are considering many paint choices, put the names into image search for design inspiration. If you are overwhelmed by the selection of colors from the start, zero in on Pinterest and Instagram. Many designers, myself included, reference paint names when we post.

AGE
APPROPRIATE

THIS PROBABLY WILL COME AS NO SURPRISE, BUT AS A CHILD I WAS very particular about what I wore. I remember one time, when I was about five years old, I came downstairs in a chunky yellow sweater with an orange, chocolate, and black stripe across the chest and caramel-colored corduroys. It was the middle of summer, and my mom said, "You gotta change that, Corey." But I also had on these oversize tangerine sunglasses, and my mom—who always really got me—understood that the glasses were nonnegotiable, so together we came up with a seasonally appropriate outfit that still worked with my artistic vision. ♟ That story says a lot about my early fixation with color and style, but it's also something I'm reminded of when I work with clients who have children. Adults usually have at least a basic idea of what kind of decor they like—romantic, traditional, modern, colorful, sleek—but when it comes to figuring out how to work their children's identities into their home design, many are at a loss. And that's a shame, because it's the children for whom that house will be particularly formative. Memories of childhood homes are often powerful and lasting. So when I'm designing a family home, I always welcome the children into the design process, interviewing them just like I do with the parents. Whether it's a sports obsession, a LEGO fixation, or unusually intense feelings about clothing, children have their preferences too, and when the decision makers take those into account, the house is more harmonious (and there's more harmony for the people living in it!). ♟ The primary space for kids in the home is, of course,

their bedrooms. And for children, the bedroom is more often a multipurpose room than it is for adults. In addition to being where they sleep, it's also where they play, study, and read. Kids can be notoriously fickle—to be fair, they are growing and changing. But there is a temptation sometimes for parents to shut down their preferences as whims or be behind the times when it comes to the Marvel superhero that is now *so* last year. A strategy I use to bridge the gap between respecting a child's stated preferences and the inevitability that those preferences will change is to satisfy them with elements that can be easily swapped out. For instance, if a child has a current favorite superhero, series of books, or sports team, try working those motifs into accessories like wall art or lamps, or use the team or character colors as the palette—wall colors aren't that hard to change—and keep the furniture (bed, dresser, desk) more neutral and less specific. That said, when it comes to color, I am perhaps a bit of a kid myself. One thing I love about working with children is that they often share my bold taste, and unlike their parents, they aren't shy about wanting to surround themselves with it!

It's important to dig deep into your children's preferences when creating spaces for studying and learning, whether that's in a bedroom or a

It's the children for whom a house will be particularly formative. Memories of childhood homes are often powerful and lasting.

dedicated study or homework nook: Do they like to do their homework sitting up straight at a desk or lying on a couch? Do they need to spread things out, or do they keep all of their papers in orderly stacks? Creating spaces that cater to the ways they prefer to work is crucial to getting good work done; if they dread going to that desk, they are going to dread homework. For the color palette, I often give a choice between blue, green, and yellow—studies have shown that those colors are conducive to concentration and retaining information.

These days, an exciting trend I am seeing is that clients are becoming more open to blurring the lines between "kid space" and "adult space." It used to be that the mantra was "I'll design my house the way I want it and confine the kids to their bedrooms." However, parents now want their children to feel more at home throughout the house or apartment, and I love finding creative ways to do that. Parents often want to showcase their children's artwork, for instance, so I treat it with the same attention and care as a valuable painting: I have wall pieces framed and matted. This communicates to children that their work is important, and as a bonus, giving those pieces some TLC will help the works last through the years and into adulthood.

PREVIOUS PAGE: The most important aspect of designing a child's room after a place to sleep is creating space to study in. If you give kids a joyful work space, they will work more diligently and creatively. Here, we painted the walls in the girl's favorite color, tangerine. One of the things I like best about working with kids is that they tend to be as fearless about color as I am. OPPOSITE: I always interview children before starting their rooms, and this wallpaper was chosen because the inhabitant said she liked butterflies. I intentionally used an elegant pattern that she wouldn't outgrow in a few years.

One of the most rewarding things about working with families is seeing how interior design can actually bring children and parents closer together. When I interview families, I always ask what kinds of things they like to do together and try to create spaces for those activities that make them even more enjoyable. One family, for instance, told me that the real debrief about everyone's day didn't take place at mealtimes but instead right before bed. So I created a special little hangout space between the owners' and children's bedrooms for them to have that cozy bonding time. I love touches like that, ones that not only respond to the family dynamics, but also help foster better relationships and lasting memories.

For children, the bedroom is a multipurpose space. In addition to being where they sleep, it's also where they play, study, and read.

RIGHT: For the bedroom of an avid reader, I created an accent wall dedicated to books. **FOLLOWING PAGES:** People often want more art but don't know where to find it. Treating your child's artwork seriously—framing it, hanging it, and showing it off to friends and family—can have a huge impact on his or her confidence and creativity. Take it from me: my mother displayed my drawings with pride in our house. In this room, the artwork drove the primary-heavy color palette.

ABOVE: Hockey—the great passion of the child whose room this is—was the driving influence in its decor. I used his favorite team's colors (red and white) and added real hockey pucks as trim. **OPPOSITE:** Sometimes people get stumped about how to decorate the corners of bedrooms. Small-scale furniture is a good way to go, and it makes sense in a kid's room. Above this play area, I made a miniature hockey rink into a light fixture. **FOLLOWING PAGES:** As with color, I find that children are more open to pattern than adults. For a little boy who loves balloons, I mixed the stripes and solids in the wallpaper with checked bedding and star-patterned stools.

THE
FUTURE
IS SO
BRIGHT

OPPOSITE: White furniture and accessories pop against the butterfly and dragonfly wallpaper. **ABOVE:** The ceiling has a polka-dot wallpaper in light pink, which provides soft contrast with the vibrant print on the walls. **FOLLOWING PAGES:** I love the challenge of creating spaces for the family: lively enough that kids want to be there, but chic enough that the parents also enjoy them. The key is using color, shape, and pattern in a way that feels youthful, but not juvenile. The walls are done in a cobalt-blue vinyl wallpaper, which is striking but also easy to clean (*left*). A cozy study nook just outside of the children's bedrooms in a family home (*right*).

LEFT: A violet room for Violet. Here, the mandate was the color, which I included several iterations of, from true violet to aubergine to a magenta rug. **ABOVE:** The touches of sage green and the organic pattern on the wallpaper bring home the botanical theme. **FOLLOWING PAGES:** A bedroom for a cultured young lady calls for a sophisticated velvet channel-back bed. While young children tend to prefer a very electric color palette, young adults, like this one, are usually a little more toned down (*left*). In this turret, I designed the homework area to accommodate a study group of friends, giving the space a hospitable, social element (*right*).

RIGHT: Another room for a young adult, with a more eclectic pattern mix: bone-inlay nightstands, a garland swag motif on the crown molding, and ikat bedding. The mirrored frames had been hung in a stairwell, and we reinvented them as a salon-style gallery.
FOLLOWING PAGES: This bedroom's study area doubles as a music practice space (*left*). A small lounge area outside a bedroom. The settee is an antique that we re-covered in durable tweed. People can be afraid to use antiques in kids' spaces, but trust me, there's nothing a kid could do to centuries-old furniture that hasn't been done (*right*).

CHANGE IT UP

Children are fickle housemates because their tastes change so rapidly as they grow.
So decorating their rooms and family spaces can be a difficult puzzle: you need to accommodate
what your kids like and do now but also anticipate their preferences down the line. My advice
is to accept this and be ready to adapt accordingly. Make strategic choices that give them some of
what they want in design elements that can be easily swapped out.

1 | FURNISH SIMPLY, AND ACCESSORIZE TO TASTE

Keep desks, dressers, and bed frames neutral, and accommodate your child's current interests
in the details. Pillows, bedding, and lamps are all relatively easy to update as your child grows.

2 | DIVIDE AND CONQUER

Wallcoverings—paint and wallpaper—are also relatively easy to change.
Consider creating an accent wall that really speaks to your kid's personality, and keep
the others a solid color. One wall is easier to redo than four.

3 | SEE THE GROWTH POTENTIAL

I love decorating kids' rooms with sports memorabilia or themes from
literature or nature, as those interests tend to be more enduring and the items can
sometimes work in other spaces if the child outgrows them.

4 | ACCOMMODATE SPRAWL

Kids rarely use family spaces in the dictionary-definition manner, so the best tactic
is to embrace multifunctionality. Consider creating a dedicated homework space in the
kitchen or using the area under a stairwell as a family reading nook.

5 | LISTENING IS KEY

In my experience, when children feel involved in the process, they are more likely
to enjoy being in the space that's designed for them. Talking to kids about what they like
and need usually yields some insight for even the most informed parents.

HAUTE HOUSE

In 2019, I was asked to design a room for the Kips Bay Decorator Show House. The room I was given had been a gentleman's study in the townhouse's original incarnation in the 1920s. In an homage to the suffragette movement and that era's early calls for equal rights, I decided to reclaim this space for women by creating an elegant, feminine room that could serve as a command center for today's chic mistress of the universe. To achieve that vision, I started by looking to contemporary fashion, one of my favorite and most trusted sources of inspiration. A recent Valentino show gave me an abundance of ideas to utilize: First, a combination of persimmon furniture, a pale pink on the walls, and jolts of green on peplum window treatments, grass cloth–covered bookshelves, and an emerald sofa, with sparkling accents, provided the color palette. Exuberant, voluminous floral-print gowns planted the seed for a floral wallcovering that I decided to use on the ceiling. Peplum dresses were translated into window treatments. ♛ I've always related to fashion design because I think I approach my work in the same way those designers do: I look back to the classic, what has been in style before, and I try to reinterpret it for the present climate with some calculated risk-taking. That's where haute house style comes in. When I start working with clients, one of the first things I pay attention to is their clothing. If a client doesn't already have an extensive design vocabulary, looking at what he or she wears gives me cues equally as valuable—if not more—to what he or she will enjoy in a home. If you like something on your body, chances are that you'll also

like seeing it on your walls, in your textiles, and on your furniture. I'll often have my clients take me into their closets and ask them to show me their favorite pieces, just in case a more conservative-looking executive secretly adores colorful prints.

So what's the process of seeing details that you like on a runway, in a magazine, or in your own closet and translating those into a home? The first step is connecting your taste in fashion elements to the realm of interiors. Do you like voluminous gowns, or do you prefer pencil skirts? That's a clue for window treatments. Do you prefer solids, abstract patterns, or representational motifs, such as florals or animal prints? That answer can give direction for fabrics and wallcoverings. Once you've oriented yourself in a personal style of likes and dislikes, you can start thinking about what overall look you are going for in each room: color-forward, or monochromatic? Tight and tailored, or more romantic and flowy? Articulating room decor in the language and visuals of apparel is a great starting point, because everyone has some sense of what he or she likes (and doesn't like) to wear.

Another cue I take from fashion is the fine line between accessorizing and junk. Just as you probably would not overwhelm a stylish outfit with all of your jewelry and tons of makeup, figuring out the right—and the right amount of—decorative accents is key to creating rooms that feel pulled together. In

Articulating room decor in the language and visuals of apparel is a great starting point, because everyone has some sense of what he or she likes to wear.

that respect, I look at designing a room like casting a movie: I always cast a lead actor and lead actress first. In other words, commit to one or two key choices, like a piece of statement furniture or a dominant color, and then carefully consider the selection of other elements in the room to make sure they support those stars. This approach can help you tamp down impulse buys, resist the trends du jour, and stay true to your original vision and taste.

Keep in mind that a fashion-inspired approach doesn't have to be "more is more." For those with a minimalist bent, I think about the articulation of silhouettes and place an emphasis on sculptural elements and crisper, more geometric shapes. To make a room feel more masculine, I often use leather furniture and accents, solid colors, and references to suit prints, like a windowpane check and pinstripes. To make a room that's more quietly feminine, I utilize softer fabrics, such as an alpaca or mohair velvet, pastel hues, and classic floral prints. While I love the copious influences and inspiration that fashion provides, I never want to bring so many of them into a room that it goes over the top. Instead I like to pick and choose my influences like selections from a box of crayons—have fun, be open to combinations, but always let your sense of personal style lead the way.

PREVIOUS PAGE: My idea for the 2019 Kips Bay Decorator Show House was to reclaim a space historically reserved for men—the gentleman's study—and reinterpret it through a fashion lens to honor the lady of the house. I brought in a nineteenth-century French Empire mahogany chair covered in a rose-colored silk and a contemporary channel-back sofa in a lush velvet. OPPOSITE: The hand-painted de Gournay wallcovering was created by an artist who also works for Buckingham Palace! The Venetian-plaster ceiling underwent an elaborate process of lacquering and torching to achieve its mirrorlike sheen.

PREVIOUS PAGES: Sometimes the best design inspiration is already built into the room. Here, the elegant grates outside the windows of the Kips Bay Library drove my choice of these Navarre chairs, whose upholstery echoes the grates. The peplum curtains were inspired by a piece from a Valentino runway show (*left*). Another inspiration was the ancient Hanging Gardens of Babylon, whose extravagance I nodded to on the ceiling with a lavish floral Cole & Son wallpaper and a midcentury French Baguès palm-tree chandelier (*right*). OPPOSITE: I really wanted this room to be an elegant homage and a chic contemporary space, so I mixed traditional decor with playful elements, such as the acrylic desk chair, the grass cloth lining the bookshelves, and the snow leopard–pattern rug. Layering artwork over bookshelves is another favorite technique of mine. RIGHT: The gilt branches on the desk clock and letter opener were another nod to the Hanging Gardens of Babylon.

LEFT: The soft color palette in this dressing space was driven by the client's taste—vanilla, champagne, and blush—and makes an ideal backdrop for trying on clothes. The flocked leopard-print wallcovering has a suede-like feel, which brings together the fashion theme with silk chandelier shades and crystal drawer pulls. FOLLOWING PAGES: An example of how restrained interior design, just like minimalist fashion, doesn't mean plain and boring. The sharp, clean lines of the bed, the nightstand (left), and the credenza (right) make a strong visual statement, which contrasts with softer elements, such as the pleated bed canopy, amber-colored grass cloth, and velvet headboard.

ABOVE: The power of fashion comes from textural nuances, like this sculptural glass-topped credenza wrapped in linen. The fabric covering the armchairs also has a fashion vibe: it would work equally well on a dress. **OPPOSITE:** Music symbolizes my love of Detroit and references my "remix" design approach, so I love building in allusions to it. **FOLLOWING PAGES:** I enjoy taking one color and using it in various hues around a room; in this owner's suite, I played with navy, cobalt, cerulean, aqua, turquoise, and sky blue. The eclectic mix of paintings and accessories is anchored by the chesterfield sofa.

LEFT: Lambrequins are a great alternative to curtains when you need structural versatility. I used one here because I had already planned an elaborate canopy treatment for the bed. The lacquer finish on the ceiling has a reflective effect that makes the room feel airier. **FOLLOWING PAGES:** The inspiration for this kitchen was an Ann Sacks tile pattern set to be discontinued. We collaborated with the brand to produce just enough for the backsplash (*left*). I painted the exposed trusses a deep espresso color to show them off. Oversize chandeliers divide this three-in-one space into zones (*right*).

OPPOSITE: The color combination of pink and green is one I fell in love with the first time I saw it on a fashion runway.

RIGHT: You can't have high fashion without the accessories. In this living room, I used oversize button details in the conversation nooks and on the ottomans, which are echoed in the pink tufted sofa. The shelves above the conversation nooks showcase art and decor objects; because of their height, I used them as display spaces rather than storage for everyday items.

FOLLOWING PAGES: Silk is synonymous with fine fashion. I upholstered these ottomans in the material to contrast their sharp, geometric shape and the ogee pattern on the fireplace grate (*left*). I reversed the strategy on my beloved peplum window treatments so the blush-colored sofa would contrast with the darker, espresso-colored part of the drapes (*right*).

OPPOSITE: I love how different fabrics behave in the light throughout the day. These chairs are actually navy, but they play like indigo when the sun hits them because of the way velvet absorbs light. **ABOVE:** Navy and white is a classic color combination in fashion, and it was perfect for a client who desired a cocoon-like bedroom. I had the walls and ceiling painted a midnight color to reserve wow-factor honors for the rose-and-vine motif on the wall behind the bed. The nightstands' sash-shaped hardware is also informed by haute couture.

RIGHT: This dining room is decked out in passementerie anchored by leather and tweed. The crystal chandelier is an antique, and the artworks had been in storage for decades; I always encourage clients to let me shop the house first before we buy something new. FOLLOWING PAGES: When fashion designers want to infuse color in a subtle way, they often use tweed. The tweed on this Roman shade allowed me to bring in all the hues of the room with an elegant, pixelated effect (*left*). The host and hostess chairs are dressed in colorful textured velvet and passementerie trim (*right*).

SPECIAL TREATMENT

Windows are some of the most costly line items in home-decor budget, so furnishing them should not be an afterthought. But that doesn't mean every window needs extravagant floor-to-ceiling drapes, only that they should be given the same careful consideration as all the other design elements in your home. If you live in a space with great architectural details, don't hide them!

1 | KNOW THE TYPES

There are four basic kinds of treatments: drapes (floor-length fabric panels), curtains (which drop just below the windowsill and are usually made from a light fabric), shades (which sit inside the window), and blinds (which are similar to shades but cover the window in slats).

2 | KNOW YOUR SPACE

Window treatments are intended to modulate the amount of light that comes into a room, so your choice should consider function and form. Drapes, for instance, are a good choice for a bedroom where you want to be able to block out all the light. However, their length makes them impractical for kitchens, where something that fits more tightly into the window is preferable.

3 | DON'T FORGET THE DETAILS

Window treatments provide a number of options for accessorizing, depending on how blinged-out you want your room to be. There are elaborate finials or more subtle, modern hardware; for more formality, you can add tassels and sashes.

4 | THE SHEER POSSIBILITIES ARE ENDLESS

Sheer drapes and curtains are often less expensive than those made from heavy fabrics, and they add levity to a room. But they aren't good at blocking light, so if you want that airy look in a place where you also need coverage, consider using a sheer fabric on top with an opaque shade or blind underneath.

5 | BUILD IN SOME STRUCTURE

For a less flowy and more tailored look, go for shades or blinds. Roman shades and roller shades have a more contemporary appearance, while blinds can be made of metal or wood.

RESOURCES

ANN SACKS • annsacks.com

ANNA SCRIPPS WHITCOMB CONSERVATORY • belleisleconservancy.org

ARTERIORS • arteriorshome.com

BAKER • bakerfurniture.com

BENJAMIN MOORE • benjaminmoore.com

BERNHARDT • bernhardt.com

BRUNSCHWIG & FILS • brunschwig.com

CARACOLE • caracole.com

CENTURY FURNITURE • centuryfurniture.com

COLE & SON • cole-and-son.com

CURREY & COMPANY • curreyandcompany.com

DE GOURNAY • degournay.com

DECORATION & DESIGN BUILDING • ddbuilding.com

DESIGN WITHIN REACH • dwr.com

DESIGNER FURNITURE SERVICES • designerfurnitureservices.com

DXV • dxv.com

EASTERN MARKET • easternmarket.org

HICKORY CHAIR • hickorychair.com

HUDSON VALLEY LIGHTING • hudsonvalleylighting.com

JUDY FRANKEL ANTIQUES • judyfrankelantiques.com

KOHLER • kohler.com

KRAVET • kravet.com

LACANCHE • lacanche.com

LA CORNUE • lacornueusa.com

LEATHERCRAFT • leathercraft-furniture.com

LEE INDUSTRIES • leeindustries.com

LEE JOFA • leejofa.com

LEFTBANK ART • leftbankart.com

MICHIGAN DESIGN CENTER • michigandesign.com

NEW YORK DESIGN CENTER • nydc.com

NEWEL • newel.com

PHILLIP JEFFRIES • phillipjeffries.com

RH • rh.com

SCHUMACHER • fschumacher.com

STEARNS & FOSTER • stearnsandfoster.com

STARK • starkcarpet.com

THE URBAN ELECTRIC CO. • urbanelectric.com

THEODORE ALEXANDER • theodorealexander.com

VISUAL COMFORT • visualcomfort.com

WATERWORKS • waterworks.com

ACKNOWLEDGMENTS

The book of Proverbs says that *"expectation postponed is making the heart sick, but the thing desired is a tree of life when it does come."* I believe this passage aptly sums up the making of *Design Remix*: it has been a tremendous—yet joyful—undertaking. And now, after years of anticipation, the reward has finally come! There are some special people who have been on this journey with me, and I would like to pay homage to them now.

First, to my editor Kathleen Jayes, for your commitment to excellence, and to Charles Miers, for your faith in my brand. Thank you both for inviting me into Rizzoli's prestigious family of authors. Caitlin Leffel, you have such an incredible gift for translating life's elements to the printed page. Susi Oberhelman, I am amazed by your artistic eye and your ability to push creative boundaries. It has been a pleasure "spinning" *Design Remix* with the four of you and the Rizzoli team at large.

To my family at Corey Damen Jenkins & Associates, both past and present, I adore you. Special thanks to Holly Selden, for keeping me sane and grounded for so many years. And to my indomitable public relations managers, Chesie Breen, Coco Van der Wolk, and Ellen Niven—you guys are quite simply the best!

To my esteemed clients: I am indebted to all of you for opening your homes and hearts with such grace and trust. It has been an absolute honor to collaborate with you over the years. I will never forget all the home-cooked meals, laughs, tears, and mutual advice on life!

Adam Wasserman, you have restored my faith in the matters of the heart. My orbit is most secure with you in it, and I struggle to articulate the depths of my appreciation for you.

Stephanie V. Gowdy, you have been my rudder during many a storm. Thank you for always telling me like it is with equal parts affection and tough love. I cherish you my dear.

Elissa Grayer, thank you for being both my gravity and the wind beneath my wings. I love you so much.

To my best friends on planet earth! Dionne Gadsden, Izzy Jimenez, Katie Harvey, Keita Turner, and Lori and Pierre Lenis: there simply are not enough words or pages available to express how deeply I love each one of you. Thank you for being there for me through the ups and downs, and for never changing.

Jamie Drake "the Great": You are the best! I am so honored by your beautiful words, kindness, and many encouraging sentiments over the years. While you reign as a legendary gatekeeper of our industry, you have always kept it real with me. Thank you for your authenticity.

To my "work moms" Patty Mulkiten, Judy Frankel, and Tracy Henbury: you were there from the very beginning. Thank you for always helping me make sense of the world.

Jody Seivert and Gloria De Lourdes Blalock, thank you for being my guiding lights.

I would also like to express gratitude to my licensing and brand partners, especially Cary and Lisa

Kravet and the Kravet family, the Stark family, and the teams at Leathercraft, DownTown Company, Benjamin Moore, Stearns & Foster, DXV, and Leftbank Art.

To Amy Astley, Doris Athineos, Maureen Feighan, Sally Finder, Ann Omvig Maine, Jeanine Matlow, Nicole Mazur, *the* Robert Rufino, Jo Saltz, Stellene Volandes, Jill Waage, and the editorial teams at *Architectural Digest* and *ELLE Decor*: you all have my eternal gratitude. Thank you for unshackling the doors for others to see my body of work. Long live print!

To my longtime photographers, Werner Straube and Brad Ziegler, for always capturing me at my best, and to Hilary Rose, Khristi Zimmeth, Barbara Winsor, and Carolyn Englefield for your camaraderie and keen eyes. George Ross, you will be sorely missed, but I take solace in knowing that you are photographing the stars of heaven now.

Ron Woodson, ten years ago your sound admonishment changed my perspective. Thank you for building my confidence to take the path less traveled as a man of color in interior design.

Alton LaDay, the genesis of this book truly started with your vision. Thank you!

Thank you to Michael Anthony Stewart, for believing in me and finding the key to door number 779.

To my many partners and friends at the Michigan Design Center, New York Design Center, and the D&D Building, huge thanks for everything!

To Gayle Wiczuk, Cathy Poses, Bruno Abbondanza, and my extended team of architects, builders, and contractors: *Design Remix* showcases some of our best work together; I appreciate you.

Special thanks to the best group of cheerleading aunts a little boy could hope for: Alesa, Bonnie, Julie, Vicki, and Marion. You rejoiced in my gains, dried my tears when I was in pain, and bolstered my courage to get out of my own way.

To my maternal grandfather, David, thank you for instilling in me a desire to wonder, ask questions, and then sketch my answers on paper. I still have all the Marvel and *Star Trek* comic books you gave me in the 1980s. Thanks for allowing me to stay up late with you to watch Johnny Carson and to feel "grown" for a minute! I will forever think fondly of our late-night chats over graham crackers and milk.

To my parents, I will always strive to be the sum of the best parts of you. Mom, you have taught me how to view the world through an optimistic lens. Dad, thank you for inculcating within me a strong sense of justice, perseverance, and a spirit of self-sacrifice. To my baby brothers, Greg and Gabriel: you were my very first best friends on earth, and I will always love you and your families.

Finally, to my beloved grandma Flossie Lee Maurant: the first time I experienced a truly broken heart was when you were suddenly taken from us. Not a single day passes by when I do not think of you. Your sage words of wisdom still resonate deeply within my soul, and they will forever guide my path forward in life. I love you.

First published in the United States of America in 2021 by
Rizzoli International Publications, Inc.
300 Park Avenue South
New York, NY 10010
www.rizzoliusa.com

Publisher: Charles Miers
Senior Editor: Kathleen Jayes
Design: Susi Oberhelman
Production Manager: Kaija Markoe
Managing Editor: Lynn Scrabis

All photography by Werner Straube Photography except:
George Ross Photography: pages 19, 40-41, 48-49, 58-77, 230-233
Marco Ricca Studio: pages 2, 205, 208-211,
David Duncan Livingston: pages 126-131, 156-163
Brad Ziegler Photography, LLC: pages 11, 14-15, 212-213
Scott Sprague Photography: pages 112-113
Beth Singer Photographer Inc.: page 83
Additional photography provided courtesy of DXV (pages 22-23) and Leathercraft Furniture (page 137)
Special thanks to Traditional Home/Meredith Corporation for the images on
the front cover and pages 6-7, 20, 24-25, 29, 30-31, 32-33, 34-35, 36-37, 38-39, 84, 96, 105, 106,
108-109, 110-111, 150-151, 152-153, 154-155, 166-167, 206, 222-223, 224-225, 226-227, 228-229

Illustrations on case, endpapers, pages 3, 16, 43, 44, 79, 80, 101, 102, 133,
134, 173, 174, 201, 202, 235: Corey Damen Jenkins
Page 12 (photo edges): Nataliia K
Pages 16, 44, 80, 102, 134, 174, 202 (paper background): Arts_Textures
Pages 16-17, 42-43, 102-103, 132-133, 134-135, 172-173 (background patterns): Sunspire
Pages 44-45, 78-79. 174-175, 200-201 (background patterns): 3Defokes
Pages 202-203, 234-235 (background patterns): Elena Zolotukhina

Printed in China

2021 2022 2023 2024 / 10 9 8 7 6 5 4 3

ISBN: 978-0-8478-6973-2

Library of Congress Control Number: 2020947634

Visit us online:
Facebook.com/RizzoliNewYork
Twitter: @Rizzoli_Books
Instagram.com/RizzoliBooks
Pinterest.com/RizzoliBooks
Youtube.com/user/RizzoliNY
Issuu.com/Rizzoli

ENDPAPERS

I drew this toile as an homage to my hometown, with each element honoring a different piece of Detroit's unique history and culture. The monument at the top left ("Campus Martius") depicts the Michigan Soldiers' and Sailors' Monument, the striking hub around which Detroit's five major thoroughfares emanate. It's a place I visit frequently to sketch and people watch. The three microphones ("House of M") represent Diana Ross and the Supremes; the harmonica below, Stevie Wonder; and the four top hats, the Four Tops—three of the most famous acts to come out of Motown, which was centered in Detroit. The roses here and elsewhere honor the residents of Detroit, who have all worked hard to earn the city its reputation: "Detroit Hustles Harder." The fountain flanked by lions depicts a beloved historic landmark in Belle Isle Park, the James Scott Memorial Fountain. I highlighted one of the lions and added a vintage car in front to symbolize how the Motor City has roared back to life, time and time again. The dome flanked by flowers, a record, and a mixtape shows the Anna Scripps Whitcomb Conservatory, a greenhouse and botanical garden to which I often retreat for drawing time or inspiration. The mixtape is a nod to my design-remix sensibility and, along with the records, headphones, and other musical details throughout, turns up the volume on Detroit's ever-thriving music scene. (In addition to Motown, it's also the birthplace of techno.) These elements reference my personal devotion to music—my staff will tell you that I never plan a room or a design a product without a good soundtrack behind me!